FLIP THE SCRIPT

Flip the Script

CHANGE YOUR THINKING, CHANGE YOUR LIFE

Shemitria Smith

The Visionary Associates

Contents

This book is dedicated to my beloved family. Your unwavering love, support, and encouragement have been the guiding light on my journey of writing this book. Your belief in me has fueled my passion and inspired me to push through every challenge. This book is dedicated to each of you, with heartfelt gratitude for your endless love and faith in my dreams. Thank you for not thinking that I was crazy when I took roads not yet paved and spoke existences not yet known.

This book is dedicated to the strong women in my life - my Mommy, my sisters, my sheros, my mentor, my hearts, my sunshines, my beautifuls. To my Black Queens, thank you for showing me how to roar. That we are the exception. That YES it is possible for me. That hard work is dreams being fulfilled. That yes, success looks like the color of my skin and not at a far away place but right here - in me, within me, around me. That we make success look like us - rare, genuine, unique, powerful. To All of my Queens, thank you for your pour. To the men in my life - my Poppa, my fathers, my brothers, my friends, my lessons, my loves, my D - thank you for standing tall. For being the example of what love is - the good and the bad. I am grateful for the past, the present and the future. Walk with the grace that you are my Kings - as you lead yourself, your future... To all my women and men, may you find the quiet, secret place that within burns the fire that conquers worlds.

To my nieces and nephews, keep pushing. To my Mommy, my Poppa - keep pushing. My shero, my heart, my sister - keep pushing. My sisterssssss - keep pushing. To my brothers - keep pushing. To my Visionaries, to the people who have really poured into my life - keep pushing. Mountains come - keep pushing. Valleys appear - keep pushing. You are strong. Trust me, I know. Even when you done gave up - keep pushing. You are more powerful than you know. We are made for greatness.

This book is dedicated to those who dare to dream, who find quiet strength in the pages of this book, and who believe in the power of words to inspire, uplift, and transform. Your imagination knows no bounds, and may this book be a companion on your journey through worlds both real and imagined. It is possible to conquer your dreams - don't give up!

Prayer, agreeance with God and acceptance of letting go and walking in obedience can go a long way. It was at one of my pivots in life God told me to just let it go. And it was hard. Because I would be letting go of a foundation that I worked so hard to build but I learned that if you are building a foundation in partnership, it has to be just that - a partnership. True bricks, true foundation comes from everybody pouring their heart into the wall of success, the wall of peace, the wall of joy, the wall of happiness that life gives us. You can't get very far without God even if you think you can do it on your own. So first, build your foundation and partnership in God.

Faith the size of a mustard seed.... what dreams can we dream. Faith the size of a mustard seed....what realities we can discover. Faith the size of a mustard seed....speak to God as if He is who you need to speak with in seeking the answers. God has placed greatness in you. Give me a moment of that time...that space...that energy.

This book is dedicated to me. To the smiling, hard-working, driven, heartbroken, scared, fearful, courageous, strong, powerful, phenomenal versions

of me that just keep pushing. I'm proud of you ma'am
- you betta gone Queen!

So, in the words of a popular company or something
like that, "Just Go Do It!" Just....go...and...do...it.
(Self always talking to self)....

Love You...I Believe in You
Shemitria

1

Sometimes the Problem is You

"My truth: I stand in my own way.
If I get over that hurdle, you can't even touch me."
– Hannah Brencher

I know just by the name of the chapter, I done lost a couple of people. But before you put the book down completely, just hear me out. Give me at least this chapter and then you can make a decision. As I was saying, rarely do we like to admit when we are in fact the problem. When yea, that was on me. I own that. I take that. Because people hardly like to acknowledge their faults. It is way easier to find fault in others versus fault in ourselves. For when we find fault with ourselves, then we have to acknowledge our flaws and life is a lot easier when acknowledging the flaws of others versus the flaws of ourselves. You know the people. The people that spend most of the days saying what they would have done if they were this person, what this person should have done, what this person isn't doing, what this person is doing, what that person should have said…I can go on and on, but the problem is, it should always be the other way around.

What are you doing, what aren't you doing, what are you saying, what aren't you saying – when you spend time critiquing, working, motivating, acknowledging and becoming aware of yourself, you will find that it leaves little room for you to focus on any other situations around you. And that's not being selfish, that is just being aware of what is important.

For years, I walked around with this book in my head. Parts of it on one computer, parts of it on another computer, losing critical data because I didn't back it up properly. Just a lot of problems and excuses that I told myself were the valid reasons why I talked about this book but had yet to produce more than a couple of chapters.

But this year, I made the decision that this year would be the year that this book would become reality. This year will be the year that I run my finger down the spine of this book. And when I made the decision, it seemed like I received steps of encouragement silently along the way. Every time I turned on the radio in the car, the words "your book is on the way" was heard. Every time I went to Bedside Baptist, the words "it is up to you to finish that book" were spoken to me over and over and over and over again. Until one day, I decided you know what, God, I think you talking to me. I think you are telling me that I need to complete this book.

But I also realized that this is not the first of these conversations either. It became the gotta complete one chapter this month, and it is vital that I have this chapter completed by this date. I had to do bite size chunks while working to stay accountable to myself. And I told a couple of people that actually held me to what I said and made me stick to my deadlines which really helped more than they know.

It became important that this become important and it had to be important enough for me to put some action, some work into making it come into fruition. I like to think that things just magically appear but I do believe that if that is possible some action has to take place to get you in that precise moment in order for the action to occur.

What if we stopped answering things we can't do, with things we can do? Instead of automatically I can't, what about I can... Most of us have already accepted failure because the "lack of" has made the final decision (and I dare to say all of us because I am sure that there is some situation that has occurred in life to make you have this moment). What if you believed that you could actually do it and thought about how you can make it happen with what you have now until you are able to fully put the plan in motion once you have all that you felt that you needed originally in order to make it happen?

What if you thought you could do 1 thing? And then grow with that one thing and add a couple more. I have a sign that hangs in my house that is right inside in the front door that says, "When you believe in yourself, anything is possible." Everything about this sign is intentional – from the placement so that it is seen every time I walk in the door to the fuel that it gives me when I sometimes doubt who I am. I also put it there so when other people walk in the door they know that anything is possible. That - thank you for allowing me to pour into you - so I do it secretively. You have to decide that yes, you can do anything that you put your mind to that you want to do, even if you have to learn how to do it.

As I have gotten older, I have realized that you can't just roam through life. It really is important to have some action toward direction or you might bump your head a few times un-necessarily (or was it just me?). You have to move with, "Lord, lead me. Guide me." The Word says that God knew you before you were born. So, you are just fulfilling his purpose for you.

When you ask Him to guide you, you begin to move with purpose and direction. Or so, this is what I have found out. And this is not a, "in order to have you have to live blameless" lesson because we all fall short, God knew we would sin but it is a moving with the intention and direction that I am moving with the thought of pleasing God.

When you move with intention, everything doesn't deserve your attention. You learn to begin to weed out the distractions and notice them, and even when you do find yourself succumbed to the distraction, you will have belief in yourself and the vision that God has given you to get up and try again. And you never know, that distraction might have actually been a part of the journey because you needed the lessons that the distraction gave you.

What would it take for you to first, acknowledge that yes you are the problem and second, take the necessary steps to walk in belief that you can accomplish your dreams. We are our own brick wall. We stand in our own way with our doubts, our insecurities, our fears, our displeasures, our lack. So, what if we remove a barrier and did it anyway. Do it scared. Do it doubtful. Do it with what you have right now. And what will happen is along the way, you will pull out the things that are already inside of you that agrees with the warrior that you are, that exemplifies the strength you carry.

You will and can believe that you are unstoppable and with the belief, the true belief, comes the action that follow. Make up in your mind today that every goal is possible! When you work from a right now mentality, you make sure that the present situation is important to the success as it pushes you forward through your goal! So choose you today, flip the script on standing in the way blocking to walking through doors of opportunities!

Discussion Questions/Action Steps:

1. Did anything in this chapter resonate with you - if you had to be honest, what do you think? Are "YOU" the problem sometimes?
2. What are some of your dreams?
3. Write your next 3 short and long terms goals that you want to accomplish in 3-6 months. Hang it on the wall next to the TV. By doing this you are showing that you believe that the things you are working toward are enough to hold yourself accountable AND by having them in writing, you will see them daily.

2

A Mindset ReSet

As a man thinketh so shall he be.
You will always act like the person you think you are.
Scripture declares, "For as a man thinketh in his heart, so is he"
(Proverbs 23:7)

What are you thinking right now? I know right – let's just jump into it once again. No, really what are you thinking right now? Is it good thoughts – have they been good thoughts an hour ago, six hours ago, when you woke up? I want you to do the first exercise of this book. I want you to take 2 minutes – set this book aside and think about what have you thought about today and then come back....

Ok, so what came to mind? So, let's talk generally first and then we will talk specifically. Were most of your thoughts about the great experiences that you have had throughout this day or did you think about what else you had to do? Did you think about the joy of taking your first breathe as you woke up this morning or did you think about what shouldn't, couldn't, or wouldn't get done. As you stood up, looked up, or shook up (ya'll know them morning shakes) did you say and believe that TODAY was going to be a good day, no, a great day because you were going to be present in the moment and live in peace and walk with God or were your thoughts on all of the problems that came, here, or are coming in the real world and in the world we live in within our mind?

It took me a really, really, really long time to say, believe and stand on these words, "Everything is going to work out according to God's purpose, which means that everything will be ok. So I have to choose to walk in peace and do my part." And that within itself is a huge responsibility because what exactly is your part.

And this is where the specifically comes in at. Can you specifically put into sections your thoughts according to your actual problems and the problems you have taken on? And how they affect the problems you already have? Which means.... Your thoughts. What are you thinking about? What are you speaking? What you speak, what you think, what you feel, what you say....what you see.

Let me repeat that and let it sink in – what you speak, what you think, what you feel, what you say…what you see. Do you believe that you are amazing? Do you believe that you are gifted, talented, special, wonderful, powerful, dynamic, inspirational and instrumental? Do you feel that you, yes you, can accomplish anything with everything that God has given you.

So, what does that mean? It means that sometimes you have to unlearn things in order to learn new things. It means that if it sounds great and wonderful coming out of my mouth, I know it will be great and wonderful when it happens in real life and I know that in order to make it happen, I have to work it with such strength as I say it out of my mouth. Don't shy away from learning, growing, stretching – which means that if you know it, speak it. The great thing about where we are right now is that we have the convenience and easy access to any platform. And what words are we speaking – to ourselves, to others?

Everybody at times tends to put their own beliefs and personas on other people and a lot of the time it is based on their belief of people. We see it all the time in everything – in good and bad. We can call them expectations. But what are the belief and persona about yourself – where do you go when you are trying to figure it out?

I have learned from personal experience that the words out of our mouth can create accountability and responsibility – rightfully so. I told myself for years that I would write this book and I ended up telling one too many people and the right people held me accountable to the fact that now you are reading a testament of me speaking things into existence.

You have the power to speak and make it happen. But the secret ingredients are God, Faith and Works. You can't say something and not move in the direction of your words. Ok, which brings us to our next exercise because I want to show you something. Would you believe me if I told you that you kinda already are speaking and making it happen. Let's go back to those thoughts and what we think about. So, let's pluck a thought out of the 50 million thoughts we think a day and say we thinking about how you just woke up "feeling" like something bad was going to happen today? And you were at work or school and had just finished a 10-page report and the power went out and you didn't save? What is the first thing that comes to mind – what do you say? I knew something bad was going to happen to me today! Or better yet, you were driving home and someone cut in front of you and you hit a pothole and got a flat tire – you knew it! You said it! (Pause) You said it....

So what if (just go with me here), what if you thought that every day was going to be a good day in some way. That nothing bad is headed your way. That great things are in store for you and they are just waiting for you to extract them out of you so that you can create great things around you. What if you decided today that today is that the day that I will no longer seek and ask for the very things that are taking me out. That with whatever I have, with whatever I am today, it will only get better and I will only speak this. I will only speak peace. I will only speak greatness. I will only speak joy. And even when the mountains come, even when the valley gets low – I will only speak God's words into, over, throughout my life because as long as I am walking, this too shall pass. As I stand right now and move, I walk with greatness, I talk with purpose, I move with direction.

Another thing about this book is that we are going to talk about some things that people may not take a liking to and that's ok. But this book is about changing our mindset so that we can change our thinking, so that we can change our life. For most of us, we have to earn money in order to have money. But this is difference with life – these next few words. YOU get to choose HOW you want to earn the money. Is it through a trade, more education, a gift, a talent – are you the next author, producer, chef, teacher or builder? Your work depends on your work. But it's not impossible and you can do it too!

Dreams are a part of us – plain and simple. It is often our connection on a spiritual level. And we all have them. From the moment we were born until I am assuming we take our last breathe, we dream when we close our eyes. But what if we dreamed with our eyes wide open or better yet make some of those dreams that are in our head a reality. I know my dreams have produced many deja-vu moments that I know for a fact is proof that I am on my purpose path – sometimes, if I may be honest and vulnerable, they come quicker in-between that I gotta go to God and be like, "what we got going on"....

But this is what I know. My reality is because of hard work…of sheer determination…of gratifying obedience. And it feels good to speak and actually see the work.

Speak what you want to see. Speak that today is a great day. And move with it. And if somebody make you mad and you let them decide that today will not be a great day for you, try again tomorrow and say "Today will be a great day!" (Maybe say it with your chest or something) And move with the feeling that TODAY WILL BE A GREAT DAY! That coffee that you love – will be extra good today. Traffic – nonexistent but if it is, find that great song and jam your way to work.

On a side note, what you will not find in this book is a lot of conversation about other people because what I want you to know is that this is between you and you. Because you choose how you walk, you choose how talk, you choose how you speak – internally and externally. You choose how you think. I will say this though, just accept that you will always be the bad person in someone else's story, and that's ok. Hey, maybe sometimes you was. We are all a work in progress.

I love you and I want us all to walk in our greatness and learn to flip the script – if we truly change our thinking, if we truly thought and walked and talked and moved with peace, we can truly change our life. And usually, into something much more than we could ever imagine or think.

Discussion Questions/Action Steps:

1. Do you think that you need a mindset reset? When was the last time you had a reset?
2. Do you find that what you speak is usually what you see?
3. Give yourself a high five tonight before you go to sleep. Just try it. You might think you are crazy - your spouse might think you are crazy - or your children might think you are crazy but trust me - try it. You are congratulating yourself for getting through today. No one else took what you took today but you did it with grace, and you might have gotten some things accomplished or anything but you made it through the day so you can even think you are giving God a high-five if you just need somebody....lol. Do it for 15 days and let me know how you feel.

3

What are You Thinking About?

"Mind is a flexible mirror, adjust it, to see a better world."
Amit Ray, Mindfulness Living in the Moment

I wanted to take another standpoint for the topic of thoughts because you have to understand how powerful your thoughts really are. I want you to stop and acknowledge that your thoughts are there and in some way, you have brought them to reality so what if you took a moment (just a moment) and delved more into this subject.

Everything starts with a thought – from the feelings that you are feeling right now to the steps you took today. Everything starts with a thought. And since you know that – what are you thinking about? I don't know if you know this, but you think

ALL DAY! Do you know the person who you talk to the most – yourself?! Some people say that the real craziness start when you talk to and answer yourself but I like to think of it as just us talking to us – me having conversation with me. Inside of us there are multiple people, multiple personalities and multiple fantasies that we are constantly interacting with. The multiple sides of me is a topic worth speaking on but I won't go deep into in this book. I just want to highlight that our chatter is constant. And for that, let's be conscious about what we are thinking about.

So where do our thoughts come from? They start with childhood learned experiences and go from heartbreak and pain to joy and peace that are experiences both externally (by other people) and internally (by ourselves). I learned a long time ago that if not careful, we will allow people to shape us and place characteristics upon us that will affect our whole lives. The key is understanding (PAUSE, now continue) that people place their projections upon you based upon the level and experience they are operating within.

Let me give you an example. If a person was involved in an abusive relationship and everything that they heard spoken to them was negative. And somehow they are able to become free from that trauma and relationship. And they don't do anything about it. A part of them to some degree has absorbed bits and pieces and what the other person has placed in them. And so, in the next relationship and with the next steps they walk within their life, they have thoughts within the negative zone. The thoughts of the characteristics that were placed within them from the past. Not knowing that they have allowed the person to subconsciously mold them. You have to get to a place of healing and discernment so that you can walk freely.

And how do you do that?! Well, most importantly, it is essential that you have a relationship with a higher power because you will need to draw strength from a power that is beyond this world to fight within and break the stigmas that have been placed on you.

You have to understand who you are – which is AMAZING!! And because you are amazing, it is only right that you think on things that resonate with power, that resonate with strength, that resonates with healing, love, joy, happiness – peace.

What if you thought that you could accomplish anything? What if you thought that you could succeed in any and everything that you do and move in the direction that when the outcome arrives, in all of its greatness, it is because you knew that through your faith that you will truly be ok.

It's so many times that I sit here and think, you know what I could be more than what I am right now. If I sit and be honest with myself, I can say that my thoughts allowed me to stop growing. My thoughts had convinced me that procrastination was my fate and I had to learn to accept it. But at some point, I decided that those thoughts were not thoughts that I wanted to fill my head. That those thoughts – the thoughts of limitation would not have the final say and therefore my feet would not have the stifleness of fear.

And I realized that I was the reason that I wasn't growing – because I wasn't doing anything to water the seed so that it could grow. In order for it to happen, I have to take steps to make it happen.

I want you to do an exercise with me. Whether you are reading or listening to this book, this is an exercise that can be done by all. I want you to take a deep breathe – breathe in a good breathe, now breathe out. Do that 2 more times. Deep breathe in, deep breathe out.

Now, I want you to tune in to your mind right now. What are you thinking about? Because I can guarantee that you are thinking. Is it positive or negative? It is encouragement or doubt? Peace or fear? And once you have identified what you are thinking about, I want you to see what steps can you take to add some positivity in that moment.

Flipping the script on your thinking can help you change how your perspective and outcome in life. Becoming aware of our thoughts help us to understand the thoughts that play in our mind, as well as, the ability to stop and place soul-filling, mind-bending, peace-keeping full and vibrant thoughts that will help us to succeed as we walk through this journey called life.

Discussion Questions/Action Steps:

1. What was the last thought you had that became a reality?
2. If you had to think about the last time you created a reality in your head from a thought, how much time did you focus on it - how did it affect you physically?
3. Have a good day today - wake up with a smile, say good morning and tell yourself even if it just for 1 day that you will have a good day. Traffic - more time to listen to something motivational before you get to it... train...good, the supplies are getting where they going so I know when I go to the store they will have plenty...extra cup of coffee - yes please! Go out of your way to have a good day...then great day...then amazing day.... Like Luther said, "If only for 1 night...." - its a work in progress but definitely achievable

4

The Way We Love

"Life is the first gift, love is the second,
and understanding is the third"
- Marge Piercy

What kind of lover are you? Will I find you searching for the perfect candle fragrance to fill the air? Or are you a have to be reminded only on Valentine celebrity? A nice dinner and movie or a Netflix and Chill type of moment huh? Well, think about it and let me know. Don't just read this book. I want you to take these words and really let them soak into you and digest as you explore within yourself.

What kind of lover are you? Notice I didn't say type because the word "type" reminds me of the word "category" which limits you to a box. No, I am asking what kind of lover are you? Which means how do you express your love outwardly? Do you openly show the joy and happiness that you are feeling? Are your physical touches handled with care and peace as you transfer energy one to another? Is it known that those around you that you say you love feel the love by your actions? And now, let me take it one step further.

What kind of lover are you to yourself? Do you inwardly feel the joy and happiness? Are the things that you ingest received as it is given with care and peace? Are you feeling love to yourself by your actions? I think as much time as we seek and look from others, it is important to seek and look within ourselves. This is when we have to take time to seek and look to and for God for guidance and direction in that quiet place. Because we know we can't stop with ourselves for the solo inner council (have you heard the thoughts that go through our head!).

We need something within us that gives us the ability to continue pushing – with love, with grace, with kindness, with joy – as we drive toward the peace that God has for us.

And maybe, just maybe, you took a moment to be honest. And within that honesty, you realized that you know what, my love is not what it could be. I am not afraid to take this moment within myself to just be open and transparent for a moment. And I know that because of the missing love inside, it kinda has manifested on the outside. And I am not so nice, not so kind, not so…but not just to people I encounter but to myself as well.

Well, first, I want you to say congratulations and bravo on being real with yourself – allowing yourself to be and accept the vulnerability. And I want you to take a deep breath. And then another one. And another one. Now place your hand over your heart. And tell yourself, "it's ok. And I know now. Now I am speaking that I am aware. And I don't like it. It's not right to others…it is not right to myself. But now that I have looked it in the face, I am deciding to make a change. I am deciding to take a first step. I am deciding that I am worthy of true love…true peace…true joy." And then, just put that in action.

But here is the thing. You have to really, really want to change. You have to really, really be committed to taking step after step in the direction that you spoke. And in your mind, what does that look like? What does true love, true peace, true joy look like? To you? For you? What steps can you take moment by moment to move toward this goal. For it is only up to you and God to get you there.

As you walk in this journey called life, I want you to know that you have the power to flip the script. You have the power to decide the words that come out of your mouth. You have the power to decide to be kind to others…to yourself. You have the power to choose to want and move and have better…within any environment. We can't control life and circumstances, but we can choose to go to God and pray and ask God to fill our hearts with love Lord, fill our minds with grace and mercy and kindness and forgiveness. And let me extend those to myself just as hard as I think I should work to extend to others. Let me work always to be the best lover to myself...and others.

You have to accept the fact that you just got to change your mind. You just have to move and put into action the flowers and trees, the birds and the bees, that everything is going to be alright. And you know what...one day, it actually will be. This doesn't mean that the finish line won't come with scars – but I promise you, it's there – just waiting for you.

Discussion Questions/Action Steps:

1. Have you ever taken a step back and thought about what kind of lover you are?
2. Who taught you what love looks like?
3. God gives us unconditional love - do you think it is possible for that kind of love to reside within you? What would that even mean for you - not to receive, but to give...

5

Validation

"We crave for the good opinion of the world, in which we don't believe, and tremble in face of its condemnation, which we despise and condemn in our hearts."
— **Hermann Sudermann**

The only validation you should strive to get acceptance from is God. I know, I know – we live in a world where validation and acceptance is a driving factor in everything around us. But and hear me out…what if you no longer felt the need to participate in society definitions (which changes often by the way – I like to call it the "roller coaster" ride). What if you made a choice and decision which stated that I choose to focus on what steps I need to take, what moves I need to make, what ideas, pouring, loving – what is it that I need to do to be validated by God?

And what does that mean – to be validated by God. I think in the most simplest terms we have to look at it the same way we look for validation and acceptance from people. We want people to believe that we are loving, kind, genuine, peaceful – and there are plenty of facts behind this because if you look at numerous reels and photos on social media, we are always presenting to the world "our best selves". It is usually a surprising caught "on-camera" moment, that people find their celebrity crushes might have a bad boy/girl side to them.

So, getting back on point, validation. Yes, I know this is a hard one because a lot of us have been conditioned unconsciously to seek and approve validations especially now that they equate to dollar signs. So, what if you thought of validation with the thought of "God, walk with me as I constantly seek and live with steps that show that your validation is one of my highest regard so lead the way."

What if you simply stopped putting so much focus on the acceptance and validation of other people. There will always people that don't like you. There will always be people that seek out your flaws. I call it misery. I say misery was so miserable it couldn't even be by itself, because misery loves company.... But what if you just chose to move the focus....move what you are giving attention to.

I know this chapter won't mean that people validation will cease to exist nor am I advocating for it to go one way or the either. I am just simply stating that for you, yes you, I would love for you to feel that worldly validation is not for you in the end all be all. Think thoughts such as, "With each grateful moment of breathe that God allows, I will use it to validate to God my gratefulness of His gift."

Also, if you feel you need to enter the world for validation, use it as a tool to validate to others their amazingness – their power. Use it to validate God's goodness in the words of love that come from our mouth or the encouragement we can provide in times of need. Use it to validate how God's Word is instruction for us and if we just take a moment to listen to God, He will provide us the validation we need when we need it.

I no longer believe in coincidences. I believe that God sends what is supposed to be sent at that moment. Whether a phone call, email, visit or text from someone who was on your mind, a song you was just thinking of in your head, people that run across your path, it is all a part of God's plan. He gives us what we need. He gives us the tools so that when we are feeling vulnerable – that when we are feeling the need to feel "accepted" or "validated" that we know where to run first.

More than anything, flipping the switch begins with flipping your mind – expanding, stretching, growing and thinking…..and thinking…and then applying. Are you a worldly validation seeker? Has social media slowly sucked you in and you gravitate toward the number of likes or shares? Whose validation are you seeking?

And I don't know if you noticed but I never talked about how there is no validation seeking whatsoever...because it is... always. Whether we want to believe it or not – even if it is seeking it from ourselves, it's there.

Discussion Questions/Action Steps:

1. Do you seek validation?
2. From Yourself or Other People?
3. Why?
4. For a full week, I want you to walk around the house, your job, at the store and say "I love and accept myself". As many times throughout the day as you can possibly remember. With clothes - or without clothes - I want you to say "I love and accept myself." And I ask, "what does that really mean?" How do you love and accept yourself? You are a masterpiece - do you believe that? What will it take for you to acknowledge the masterpiece that you are?

6

Don't Hate Your Past, to Look Forward to Your Future

"Forget what hurt you but never forget what it taught you"
– Shannon L. Alder

Many of us tell ourselves all the time that if we had of made that other decision, or chosen a different path our life would have turned out completely different that it would have been. Which to some degree is the truth. But you don't know for certain if that path would have been better, been worse, or landed you still exactly where you are. This is where faith comes in. You have to believe that God brought you through what He brought you through so that you can be at this moment right now.

Though painful as they may have been, it was in the worse times that some of our strongest strengths have been born. We never know how strong we are until strength is our only choice. And decide to choose it over and over again. Choose strength in the present....choose thanks for the past. The past is just what it is..the past. You can't change any of it. How it happened is how it happened. This is where choice comes in.

SO now, you have to choose to decide if you are going to live in your past and constantly regret your decisions and relive them over and over again, or are you going to choose to only remember the past to appreciate the lessons that it taught you as you move toward your future. But here is the thing, you don't have to hate your past in order to move forward. You don't have to hate your past in order for you to change. You don't have to hate your past to be happy about what it is ahead.

Never be ashamed of any moment in your life that you have had. Because it those moments that have made us who we are. And I don't know about you. But I am glad to be who I am. Am I happy about many of the situations I have found myself in based off a lot of the choices I have made? No, absolutely not. BUT I do appreciate those hard lessons because they have made me who I am today.

They have made me realize that some things are worth more choosing than others. Like peace. Listen, we all make mistakes. No one, certainly not me, is saying that in order to have to have a fantastic future you have to be perfect. No. Please don't think that is what I am saying. I am saying that life is lesson, it has its ups and downs, highs and lows, successes and failures. What I am saying is what the great Les Brown says, "Practices make IMPROVEMENT not PERFECTION because perfection is unattainable."

As long as you are realizing and accepting and forgiving and loving the parts about your past that wasn't so great, also appreciate the lessons as they help you shape your future. Understand, we are who we are. Which without our past, we wouldn't be who we are. So if you do not like who you are, use your past to shape you to be who you are. Your past is a tool. A tool to help you walk toward your purpose, your destiny that God has for you.

Your past if anything, should help you to make better choices, if that is what you want your future to be about. And be honest about your past - some people, some experiences - was not bad. And things didn't end because it was bad. Some people in my life have implanted treasures deep inside of me that I will treasure for the rest of my life. And for that, I will always have love for them. Some roads take different turns based off growth - and that is ok because seasons come and seasons go - it is about being honest especially if you are no longer growing.

Someone used to tell me all the time – practically scream it in my face. "The definition of insanity is the doing the same thing over and over again expecting a different result." Read that again. The DEFINITION of INSANITY is DOING the SAME thing Over and Over Again EXPECTING a DIFFERENT result.

Stop. Stop what you are doing right now and think about the many times throughout your life you have basically been INSANE over something. I keep eating fast food over and over again – I can't understand why I'm not healthy. I keep half-exercising, but I can't understand why I'm not fit. I keep procrastinating on writing this book, but I can't understand why it isn't my words inspiring people. I keep sleeping in and laying around, but I can't understand why I don't life is so hard for me. I can't I can't I can't because I'm not I'm not I'm not. You CANNOT keep doing the same thing over and over again and expecting a different result.

You have to flip the script. You have to think differently. Last time I checked, I wasn't getting a check for my mental health – what about you? Not in terms of whether I was implying insanity upon my own situation by my own doing. Life sometimes can be a hard pill to swallow. But sometimes we learn within those hard pills we swallow, something else is developed. Someone else emerges. We are pushed. We are pulled.

A stronger version of who we are emerges, this strength only unleashed by the cries of desperation, frustration and repetitive pain. But the stronger version brings clarity that was shielded, understanding that surpasses all and direction that was clouded. Learn to flip the script, even if only for a moment, and be amazed at what lessons you can learn to derive from the past to appreciate not only that experience but anticipated hope for the future. So thank the past - give the past its flowers. Celebrate it, appreciate it and walk with purpose toward the future.

Discussion Questions/Action Steps:

1. Have you accepted that your past has happened and you cannot change it?
2. How many times throughout the day do you change the story and think the present would be different if Option B was chosen?
3. Learn to find the beauty in the lessons of the past. Don't just put the spotlight on the "bad" things.... seek what the value of the time was supposed to be as you pour into the concrete of today.

7

Forgiveness

"True forgiveness is when you can say,
thank you for the experience."
– Oprah Winfrey

Some things are much easier said than done. Which means some things sound great when they come out of your mouth but actually putting action behind them – well, you may be doing too much there – lol. It took me a while to even write this chapter because I stand firm behind the words I say so if I am going to say this, then I have to walk it as well. Forgiveness is hard. It's hard because it is personal. When people hurt you, when people do you wrong, when people disrupt your peace, your joy – then it is hard to say, you know what I forgive you.

I heard a message tonight and the messenger of God spoke about grace and mercy toward someone that did you wrong. He said that forgiveness is at the forefront of how we move, how we live, how we pray, how we extend grace and mercy. And it made me question myself to ask – no, let me clarify that and be honest, it made me acknowledge the fact that yes, there are people in my life that I have yet to forgive. To me, the justification is the level of maliciousness, intent, and trifleness was inflicted upon me. And as he was praying, as I was praying, I was asking God to show me those I have allowed to stand in the way of my grace and mercy by my silent, unrelenting act to forgive.

I went from my knees to the ground as God uncovered me...exposed me. And it was then and there, as he allowed the unspoken grudge to come to mind, I allowed forgiveness to wash over me. I asked God to forgive me as I openly forgave others for the acts of injustice to me. I thanked God for allowing me to have the opportunity to have this moment. For I wasn't on my death bed or in a hospital bed but in an environment where I am free – free to move forward. Free to keep pressing toward my goals. Free to flip the script and move with intention.

Some of us may be thinking that maybe there should be some exceptions to the rule on a case-by-case basis perhaps. Or the hurt inflicted upon you is not worth the level where forgiveness is even an option in the situation. Well, I am here to tell you – there is forgiveness in everything and everyone – in every situation in every bone.

Forgiveness extends to everything. E V E R Y T H I N G. And trust, this was hard for me to because I consider myself a good person in the sense that I live to pour nothing but goodness into the people that God blesses across my path. And I walk with the thought and notion that because I spread it, if you are around me in my closeness, those actions would be reciprocated but life has shown me that this is not the case. And life has shown me just how menacing, selfish actions can be in the name of love wrapped in hurt and pain. Scenarios of mistrust that I can prove my case in why forgiveness would be justified in not giving.

But in all honesty, it doesn't really matter. Unforgiveness is us doing to us what bad intention people do to other people - inflict pain. Hurt people hurt people. So if you are hurting inside because you are not forgiving, you are hurting yourself. You block grace and mercy to flow down to you.

Yes, it will come and yes, it might even be plentiful and abundantful BUT I firmly believe that if true forgiveness was spoken upon and followed through with the walk, the prosperity that comes from the Lord will come at magnitude speeds.

Also, remember in the moments of forgiveness, where you are finding areas of unspoken unforgiveness to release, don't forget to look at the spaces within yourself. Move, think and pray with the intention of giving yourself grace, mercy and forgiveness for not the best choices, ideas, thoughts, actions.

Open yourself up to receive the love that is within you – remove the blocks. Today, I want you to openly forgive. Openly forgive. Openly forgive. Make room for the grace and mercy that will follow.

I take a pause right here because before you move on to the next chapter, I want you to stop right here and take the rest of the day or night to talk to God and ask him to expose you – to the unforgiveness. And ask him to grant you the grace and mercy to not only call the people to name but bring the situation to the forefront so that you can acknowledge it, forgive it and release it.

Attach the pain to the situation and remove the parts where bitterness resides. If you have to look at the situation, learn to look for the lessons within (and not the neck-rolling ones) – but those lessons that inspired you for better.

Ask God to forgive you for holding onto the anger because you acknowledge that because you made the choice to hold on, you made the choice to block God to flow through you. Release what no longer serves you so that you can fill it with what God has in store for you. You are more powerful than what you give yourself the acceptance to know.

You are a masterpiece – fierce and strong. So forgive hero! We are all in this together! I read this to myself too! We are all a work in progress

Discussion Questions/Action Steps:

1. True submission to God is when we learn to exercise forgiveness. If we actively worked toward forgiveness, how many people would you be willing to truly release and forgive?
2. Forgiveness of self is just as important as forgiveness of others. Spend some time with you and truly releasing and forgiving yourself in those moments, those emotions, truly release that space that you have been holding against yourself.
3. Forgiveness can stem from being around others where the environment causes a reason for forgiveness - what steps can you take to not even be in the space for the use of forgiveness to be given? What other avenues are waiting for you to stroll down?

8

What are You Grateful for?

"The most powerful weapon against your daily battles
is finding the courage to be grateful anyway." – Unknown

Every morning when I become alert and realize that I am no longer sleep, I start thanking God. I begin the moment with gratitude. As I arise and get out the bed and move around, I speak gratefulness and thanks and appreciation to God for allowing me to function on my own.

Even before I think about the day, the people, the frustrations, the drama – I take real moments to just be grateful. I take real moments to just appreciate that I have – that I have the ability to hear, to speak, to think, to move, to see, to walk, to talk, to just be. Because it is in those moments that I realize that as much as things could be wrong, there are just as many things that are right. There are just as many things that are happening in my favor.

Would you believe me if I told you that "stress" is magic – or mythical? Why – because can you show me stress in physical form. When trials happen, when we go through things – the situation may cause us to display physical results of what stress does to our mind and body, but stress itself isn't the cause. Stress is never the cause - only a symptom of our thoughts. Images we have created in our head, create a physical degrading of our body, our mind, our soul. We instantly think defeat.. failure. Does that sound like you?

I know. I have been there. Depending on the situation, the day, the hour - I may find myself in that place again. But I don't stay there very long. Because I learned how to be grateful. I mean really grateful. I learned to thank God for what I do have. I learned to thank God for my health, my strength, the solution, the clarity, the wisdom, the understanding, the Word, His grace. I start focusing on possibilities...opportunities... Why?

Because if I have to focus on anything, I would rather focus on things that will empower me, uplift me, encourage me – gratitude. I rather focus on appreciating what I do have. I am grateful for small things, as well as, the big things. And when I think of gratefulness the first thing that doesn't come to mind is material, even though I am grateful for that.

But what comes to mind is gratefulness for a sane mind, gratefulness for the ability to get up and go for myself – by myself. The ability to count so I know what my dollars looking like (lol).

There is something in every moment to be grateful for. For when you find the time to be grateful, you will continue to grow and be greatful. Openly participating in acknowledging gratefulness in your life is a great step each moment in flipping the switch. When things become burdensome and you seem like life can't get any worse, stop, breathe, and take a moment to be grateful for that breathe. And then look around, take that moment to be grateful for the ability to look around, the ability to notice the browning of the leaves in the trees (if its Fall where you are like me) or the greenness of the grass.

Just take a moment, place it over your heart and just bask in the gratefulness. I guarantee you if you actively practice this, you will begin to appreciate the small things and the larger things will begin to fall into place.

The best feeling in the world is to be alive. I am so grateful to be alive. I am grateful for my eyes, legs, arms, fingers, toes, mouth, teeth, head, brain, skin, underwear, taste buds, ears. I am grateful for the ability to experience peace. I am grateful that I have the space, the environment around me to create, to pray, to walk, to think, to dream, to feel, to be. I am grateful that I have had the chance to experience the moment that I know that God has brought me over.

I am grateful that everything is going to be ok, so I am grateful that I am able to get up and keep moving in whatever fashion that looks like.

What will it look like to you, for you, with you and around you to walk in the wholeness of gratefulness? When genuineness flows out of your heart, it is because you can experience the greatfulness that is stored/poured within you by God. Learn to flip the script and tap into the power that is already in you.

Discussion Questions/Action Steps

1. Sometimes we can complain about something so much, that we forget that it was once something we prayed for. What action steps can we take to infuse the gratefulness that we once felt back into the picture?
2. If we walk in a spirit of gratefulness, how do we show up? Is it with a smile - is it with the energy to get it, an air of expectancy of the greatness of the day?
3. For the next 7 days, I want you to wake up in the morning and speak 10 things you are grateful for. I will start you off - thank you Lord for my legs, my arms, my eyes, my ears, my hands... and there you go - go from there. This promotes an air of thankfulness when we first inhale because He gave us importantly breathe and fortunately, the resources and tools to make it through the day. And

even if you are missing some or more of these things, there is always something to be grateful for - because you are breathing.

4. Can you accept that your gratuity is not as high based on the steps you are taking right now? How can you move differently so that you can acknowledge true gratefulness as it is and walk in it.

9

Thank You

When thinking of how I wanted this book to end, it took me a while to come to this conclusion because the #1 question that was on my brain was, "what is the message that I want people to ingest?" I knew that I wanted a book that will inspire and spark a fire. I didn't want something super long because I don't think that it took 800,000 words in order for you to get what you needed but the doubtful part in me felt exactly that way and hindered me for years, honestly. I wanted something anybody can pick up – young, old, male, female – and find something hidden within the pages that they were waiting to hear.

This is not an overnight success. This is not a get rich quick book. But this is a pivotal moment piece of art that if read with an open mind can transform your life. Listen, don't just plow through this book. Actually take the time and read it. And think about it. Read a chapter a day or week and let the words sink into you where you can see where something off the page can be implemented. This is a, "I needed that reminder or I needed those words" type of book. This book was written purely in love because we are all great. It's the walking in the greatness that is the hard work, but we doing hard any way right. Sending you love, peace and abundance energy as you walk in your journey!

I would LOVE to hear from you - you can email me at contact@thevisionaryassociates.com! Did this book pour into you? How did the implemented techniques show up in your life – your language? Follow us at @TheVisionaryAssociates on social media (Facebook, Instagram) to leave a comment AND keep up to date on our life coaching sessions, vision board workshops, transformational summits and our very own Positivity Possession course.

Shemitria is the Founder & CEO of The Visionary Associates, a company that specializes in helping people find their passion through self-development. Many clients have self-benefited from her vision board workshops. Shemitria holds a Masters of Education in Organizational Leadership from American InterContinental University. She has also taken Executive Programs offered by the Harvard Business School. It is her goal to press forward to obtain her Doctorate in Leadership in 2025.

Shemitria loves to spend her down time with the ocean as her background. It helps her to understand just how limitless God is - how vast He is when you see nothing but water to the left and right of you.....You got this, I believe in you. Now, you believe in you. God made you rare.